WORKBOOK

For

The Well-Lived Life

A 102-Year-Old Doctor's Six Secrets to Health and Happiness at Every Age

[A Guide to Implementing Gladys McGarey's Book]

Kelly Press

Table of Content

How To Use This Workbook 4

Overview 6

SECRET I: YOU ARE HERE FOR A REASON 7

Key Lessons...7

Action Prompts 9

SECRET II: ALL LIFE NEEDS TO MOVE...........................16

Key Lessons..16

Action Prompts 18

SECRET III: LOVE IS THE MOST POWERFUL MEDICINE .25

Key Lessons..25

Action Prompts 27

SECRET IV: YOU ARE NEVER TRULY ALONE 34

Key Lessons..34

Action Prompts 36

SECRET V: EVERYTHING IS YOUR TEACHER 43

Key Lessons 43

Action Prompts 45

SECRET VI: SPEND YOUR ENERGY WILDLY...................52

Key Lessons 52

Action Prompts 54

Learning Review Questions 61

How To Use This Workbook

This workbook provides you with the chance to investigate a variety of aspects of your life, identify areas in need of improvement, and observe your advancement. It has a compilation of essential topics, questions to stimulate contemplation, and learning review questions to gauge your progression.

To ensure you stay on track and make progress, it's advised that you establish a timeline for completing the workbook. Set aside specific periods to work through the prompts and learning review questions. This will help you maintain your momentum and ensure you make steady progress.

The workbook commences with a short recap of the main book, acquainting you with the topic discussed in the title. This approach is highly beneficial for obtaining a deeper understanding of the content covered in the workbook, as well as identifying the areas that require the most attention.

The key lessons and the action prompts provided in this workbook aim to inspire contemplation on various facets of your life. You need not respond to all of them simultaneously and may revisit them later. They serve as a base for your self-reflection and personal exploration.

Once you complete the activities in this workbook, you can assess your progress by answering self-assessment questions. The purpose of these questions is to prompt you to reflect on your learning and identify which areas you need to focus on more. Armed with this knowledge, you can devise effective strategies to enhance your comprehension of the material.

Feel free to spend enough time on the prompts and self-assessment questions. You do not need to finish them in one go. You can take a pause and come back to them later. The most significant thing is to be truthful to yourself and to give careful thought to your responses.

Good luck!

Kelly Press

Overview

Dr. Gladys McGarey's book The Well-Lived Life: A 102-Year-Old Doctor's Six Secrets to Health and Happiness at Every Age gives practical advice on how to live a satisfying life at any age. Dr. McGarey is a holistic physician who has been in practice for almost 70 years and has survived to be over 100 years old.

She discusses six secrets in this book that she feels are crucial for living a fulfilling life. These include the value of family and community love and support, staying physically active, eating a healthy diet, finding purpose and meaning in life, being flexible and adaptable, and having spiritual practice.

Dr. McGarey illustrates her ideas with tales from her own life and medical practice, as well as practical advice and activities to help readers incorporate her insights into their own lives. The book provides readers of all ages and backgrounds with a comprehensive approach to well-being.

The Well-Lived Life is a motivational book that urges readers to nurture love, purpose, adaptability, and trust in their everyday lives.

SECRET I: YOU ARE HERE FOR A REASON

Key Lessons

1. The importance of finding purpose: According to Dr. McGarey, everyone has a unique purpose and reason for being here. She encourages readers to discover their own purpose in life and pursue it with passion and dedication.

2. The benefits of service to others: Dr. McGarey emphasizes the importance of serving others and finding ways to make a positive impact in the world. She believes that serving others is not only beneficial for the recipients of the service, but also for the person providing it.

3. The role of attitude in finding purpose: Dr. McGarey believes that having a positive attitude is essential for finding one's purpose in life. She encourages readers to cultivate a sense of gratitude and appreciation for life, and to approach challenges with a growth mindset.

4. The power of visualization: Dr. McGarey suggests that readers visualize themselves achieving their

goals and living their purpose. She believes that visualization can help people stay focused and motivated, and can bring their goals closer to reality.

5. The importance of self-reflection: Dr. McGarey encourages readers to regularly reflect on their lives and their progress towards their goals. She suggests journaling or meditating as ways to facilitate self-reflection, and believes that self-awareness is essential for living a well-lived life.

Action Prompts

Have you taken the time to consider what your unique purpose or calling in life might be? If not, what steps could you take to explore this further?

_____

_____

_____

_____

_____

_____

_____

_____

_____

_____

_____

_____

_____

In what ways could you serve others and make a positive impact in the world? How might this benefit both others and yourself?

_____

_____

_____

_____

_____

_____

_____

_____

_____

_____

_____

_____

_____

_____

_____

How would cultivating a more positive attitude help you to find and pursue your purpose in life?

_____

_____

_____

_____

_____

_____

_____

_____

_____

_____

_____

_____

_____

Have you tried visualizing yourself achieving your goals and living your purpose? If not, how might you incorporate visualization into your daily routine?

_____

_____

_____

_____

_____

_____

_____

_____

_____

_____

_____

_____

_____

_____

How often do you reflect on your life and your progress towards your goals? What methods of self-reflection have you found to be most effective?

_____

_____

_____

_____

_____

_____

_____

_____

_____

_____

_____

_____

_____

What challenges or obstacles have you encountered while pursuing your purpose, and how have you overcome them?

_____

_____

_____

_____

_____

_____

_____

_____

                       .

_____

_____

_____

_____

_____

_____

What role does gratitude and appreciation play in your life? How might focusing on gratitude help you to find and pursue your purpose?

_____

_____

_____

_____

_____

_____

_____

_____

_____

_____

_____

_____

_____

SECRET II: ALL LIFE NEEDS TO MOVE

Key Lessons

1. Exercise doesn't have to be strenuous to be effective: Dr. McGarey notes that physical activity can take many forms, and it's important to find something that you enjoy and that fits your lifestyle. Even light exercise like walking or gardening can have significant health benefits.

2. Moving your body helps your mind: Dr. McGarey explains that physical activity can have a positive impact on mental health, reducing stress and anxiety and improving cognitive function. Exercise can also help prevent age-related cognitive decline.

3. Sitting is the new smoking: Dr. McGarey points out that sedentary behavior, such as sitting for extended periods, has been linked to numerous health problems, including heart disease, obesity, and diabetes. She encourages readers to find ways to incorporate movement into their daily routines, such as taking regular breaks to stand or stretch.

4. Consistency is key: Dr. McGarey emphasizes the importance of regular exercise for overall health and well-being. She recommends finding a physical activity that you enjoy and making it a regular part of your routine, whether that means daily walks or regular yoga classes.

5. Movement is a lifelong habit: Dr. McGarey believes that staying physically active is essential for health and happiness at every age. She encourages readers to view exercise as a lifelong habit and to find ways to stay active no matter what their age or physical abilities may be.

Action Prompts

What physical activities do you enjoy, and how can you incorporate them into your daily routine?

_____

_____

_____

_____

_____

_____

_____

_____

_____

_____

_____

_____

_____

_____

How much time each day do you spend sitting, and what changes can you make to be more active throughout the day?

_____

_____

_____

_____

_____

_____

_____

_____

_____

_____

_____

_____

_____

_____

What benefits do you personally experience from regular physical activity, and how can you use these benefits as motivation to stay active?

_____

_____

_____

_____

_____

_____

_____

_____

_____

_____

_____

_____

_____

_____

Are there any physical activities you've been meaning to try but haven't yet? How can you make time to explore new activities that might become enjoyable habits?

_____

_____

_____

_____

_____

_____

_____

_____

_____

_____

_____

_____

_____

_____

How do you feel when you go for long periods without moving your body, such as when sitting at a desk all day? How can you create more opportunities for movement in your day to avoid these feelings?

_____

_____

_____

_____

_____

_____

_____

_____

_____

_____

_____

_____

_____

What physical activities do you enjoy doing with others, and how can you create opportunities to exercise with friends, family, or coworkers?

_____

_____

_____

_____

_____

_____

_____

_____

_____

_____

_____

_____

_____

How has your physical activity level changed over time, and what factors have contributed to these changes?

_____

_____

_____

_____

_____

_____

_____

_____

_____

_____

_____

_____

_____

SECRET III: LOVE IS THE MOST POWERFUL MEDICINE

Key Lessons

1. Love and connection are essential for good health: Dr. McGarey emphasizes the importance of having strong relationships with family, friends, and community. She believes that love and support are essential for overall health and happiness.

2. Loneliness can have negative health consequences: According to Dr. McGarey, loneliness can have negative health consequences, including increased risk of heart disease, depression, and cognitive decline. It is important to cultivate meaningful connections with others to avoid the negative effects of loneliness.

3. Forgiveness is a powerful form of love: Dr. McGarey emphasizes the importance of forgiveness in relationships. Holding onto anger and resentment can have negative effects on health, and forgiveness is a powerful form of love that can promote healing and improve relationships.

4. Love can help heal physical and emotional pain: According to Dr. McGarey, love can help heal both physical and emotional pain. Love and emotional support can help reduce pain and promote healing after illness or injury.

5. Love is contagious: Dr. McGarey emphasizes that love is contagious and can spread from person to person, promoting positive feelings and behaviors. By cultivating love and connection in our own lives, we can contribute to a more loving and connected world.

Action Prompts

How important are your relationships with family, friends, and community to your overall health and happiness?

_____

_____

_____

_____

_____

_____

_____

_____

_____

_____

_____

_____

_____

Have you experienced loneliness in your life? How has it affected your health and well-being?

_____

_____

_____

_____

_____

_____

_____

_____

_____

_____

_____

_____

_____

_____

Is there someone in your life whom you need to forgive in order to promote healing and improve your relationship?

_____

_____

_____

_____

_____

_____

_____

_____

_____

_____

_____

_____

_____

Have you ever experienced the healing power of love and emotional support during a time of physical or emotional pain?

_____

_____

_____

_____

_____

_____

_____

_____

_____

_____

_____

_____

How can you cultivate more love and connection in your own life, and contribute to a more loving and connected world?

_____

_____

_____

_____

_____

_____

_____

_____

_____

_____

_____

_____

_____

Have you ever witnessed the contagious nature of love and positive emotions in others? How did it make you feel?

_____

_____

_____

_____

_____

_____

_____

_____

_____

_____

_____

_____

_____

How can you prioritize love and connection in your life, and make it a central focus of your daily actions and relationships?

_____

_____

_____

_____

_____

_____

_____

_____

_____

_____

_____

_____

_____

_____

SECRET IV: YOU ARE NEVER TRULY ALONE

Key Lessons

1. Finding purpose and meaning in life is essential for overall well-being. According to Dr. McGarey, having a sense of purpose is as important for physical health as it is for mental health. She encourages readers to find activities and pursuits that bring them joy and fulfillment, whether it's a hobby, a career, or a volunteer opportunity.

2. Don't be afraid to pursue your passions. Dr. McGarey believes that it's never too late to pursue your passions and find purpose in life. She shares stories of individuals who have found their true calling later in life and encourages readers to follow their hearts.

3. Your purpose may change throughout your life. Dr. McGarey emphasizes that purpose is not a fixed thing and may evolve over time. She encourages readers to be open to new experiences and to reevaluate their goals and aspirations periodically.

4. Service to others can bring a sense of purpose. Dr. McGarey believes that serving others can bring a sense of purpose and meaning to life. She encourages readers to find ways to help others, whether it's through volunteering or simply being kind to those around them.

5. Finding purpose can improve overall health and happiness. Dr. McGarey believes that finding purpose can improve overall health and happiness, and she cites research to support this claim. She encourages readers to take the time to reflect on their values and goals and to make purposeful choices in their daily lives.

Action Prompts

What are your passions and how have you pursued them to find purpose in life?

_____

_____

_____

_____

_____

_____

_____

_____

_____

_____

_____

_____

_____

_____

How do you remain open to new experiences and evaluate your goals and aspirations over time?

_____

_____

_____

_____

_____

_____

_____

_____

_____

_____

_____

_____

_____

In what ways have you helped others and found a sense of purpose through service? How has this impacted your own well-being?

_____

_____

_____

_____

_____

_____

_____

_____

_____

_____

_____

_____

_____

How do your values and priorities shape your daily choices and actions? How do they contribute to a sense of purpose in your life?

_____

_____

_____

_____

_____

_____

_____

_____

_____

_____

_____

_____

_____

_____

What activities and pursuits bring you joy and fulfillment? How can you incorporate more of these into your daily routine?

_____

_____

_____

_____

_____

_____

_____

_____

_____

_____

_____

_____

_____

_____

How do you see the connection between having a sense of purpose and overall health and happiness in your own life?

_____

_____

_____

_____

_____

_____

_____

_____

_____

_____

_____

_____

_____

What steps can you take to cultivate a deeper sense of purpose and meaning in your life, and what barriers do you anticipate in this process?

_____

_____

_____

_____

_____

_____

_____

_____

_____

_____

_____

_____

_____

_____

SECRET V: EVERYTHING IS YOUR TEACHER

Key Lessons

1. Learning from difficult situations: Dr. McGarey encourages readers to view challenging situations as opportunities for growth and learning. She believes that difficult experiences can teach us important lessons and help us develop resilience and strength.

2. Cultivating a growth mindset: Dr. McGarey emphasizes the importance of having a growth mindset, which means viewing challenges and setbacks as opportunities for learning and improvement. She encourages readers to embrace a mindset of curiosity and to approach life with a sense of openness and wonder.

3. Appreciating the present moment: Dr. McGarey believes that every moment is an opportunity for learning and growth. She encourages readers to be fully present in each moment and to appreciate the beauty and wonder of life.

4. Practicing gratitude: Dr. McGarey emphasizes the importance of cultivating a sense of gratitude and appreciation for life. She encourages readers to focus on the positive aspects of life and to be thankful for the blessings they have.

5. Learning from others: Dr. McGarey believes that everyone we meet can teach us something valuable. She encourages readers to be open to learning from others and to seek out mentors and teachers who can guide them on their path to growth and self-discovery.

Action Prompts

How do you typically respond to difficult situations? Do you see them as opportunities for growth and learning, or do you tend to get discouraged or overwhelmed?

In what ways do you cultivate a growth mindset? Do you approach challenges with a sense of curiosity and openness, or do you tend to get stuck in negative thought patterns?

_____

_____

_____

_____

_____

_____

_____

_____

_____

_____

_____

_____

_____

_____

How often do you take the time to appreciate the present moment? Are you able to find joy and wonder in the simple things in life, or do you tend to get caught up in worries and stress?

_____

_____

_____

_____

_____

_____

_____

_____

_____

_____

_____

_____

_____

_____

How do you practice gratitude in your daily life? Do you make a conscious effort to focus on the positive aspects of your life, or do you tend to take things for granted?

_____

_____

_____

_____

_____

_____

_____

_____

_____

_____

_____

_____

_____

_____

How open are you to learning from others? Do you seek out mentors and teachers who can guide you on your path to growth and self-discovery, or do you tend to rely solely on your own knowledge and experience?

_____

_____

_____

_____

_____

_____

_____

_____

_____

_____

_____

_____

_____

_____

What role does self-reflection play in your life? Do you regularly take time to reflect on your experiences and learn from them, or do you tend to stay stuck in old patterns of thought and behavior?

_____

_____

_____

_____

_____

_____

_____

_____

_____

_____

_____

_____

_____

_____

How do you respond to feedback and criticism from others? Do you see it as an opportunity for growth and learning, or do you tend to get defensive and closed off?

SECRET VI: SPEND YOUR ENERGY WILDLY

Key Lessons

1. Find a spiritual practice that resonates with you: Dr. McGarey emphasizes that spirituality is a personal journey and that each individual must find a practice that resonates with them. This could be through organized religion, meditation, prayer, or other forms of spirituality.

2. Cultivate gratitude and appreciation: Dr. McGarey encourages readers to cultivate gratitude and appreciation for life. She suggests starting each day with a moment of gratitude and focusing on the positive aspects of life.

3. Practice forgiveness: Dr. McGarey emphasizes the importance of forgiveness in cultivating spiritual well-being. She suggests letting go of grudges and resentments and focusing on forgiveness and compassion towards oneself and others.

4. Connect with nature: Dr. McGarey believes that connecting with nature is a powerful way to cultivate spiritual well-being. She suggests

spending time in nature, whether it be hiking, gardening, or simply sitting outside and appreciating the natural world.

5. Share your energy with others: Dr. McGarey encourages readers to share their positive energy with others. She suggests volunteering or finding ways to give back to the community, as this can be a powerful way to connect with something greater than oneself and find purpose and meaning in life.

Action Prompts

Have you found a spiritual practice that resonates with you? If not, what steps can you take to explore different spiritual practices and find one that aligns with your values and beliefs?

_____

_____

_____

_____

_____

_____

_____

_____

_____

_____

_____

_____

_____

_____

How often do you take time to cultivate gratitude and appreciation for life? What are some ways you can incorporate gratitude into your daily routine?

_____

_____

_____

_____

_____

_____

_____

_____

_____

_____

_____

_____

Are there any grudges or resentments you are holding onto? How can you practice forgiveness and compassion towards yourself and others?

How often do you spend time in nature? What are some ways you can prioritize connecting with the natural world in your daily life?

_____

_____

_____

_____

_____

_____

_____

_____

_____

_____

_____

_____

Have you considered volunteering or finding ways to give back to your community? If not, what are some ways you can use your energy to make a positive impact on those around you?

_____

_____

_____

_____

_____

_____

_____

_____

_____

_____

_____

_____

_____

_____

What role does spirituality play in your overall well-being? How can you deepen your spiritual practice and connect with something greater than yourself?

_____

_____

_____

_____

_____

_____

_____

_____

_____

_____

_____

_____

_____

_____

How can you share your positive energy with others in your daily life? What are some small ways you can uplift those around you and contribute to a more positive and supportive community?

_____

_____

_____

_____

_____

_____

_____

_____

_____

_____

_____

_____

_____

Learning Review Questions

What made you purchase this workbook?

_____

_____

_____

_____

_____

_____

How have you been using the workbook so far?

_____

_____

_____

_____

_____

_____

What do you feel you have gained from using the workbook?

_____

_____

_____

_____

_____

_____

How has the workbook helped you to achieve your goals?

_____

_____

_____

_____

_____

_____

Are there any parts of the workbook that were particularly helpful or challenging for you?

_____

_____

_____

_____

_____

_____

_____

How has your understanding or knowledge of the topic changed since working through the workbook?

_____

_____

_____

_____

_____

_____

How do you plan to continue using the workbook or incorporating the information in your life?

_____

_____

_____

_____

_____

_____

_____

Made in the USA
Middletown, DE
14 June 2023